# BECOMING GOD'S WOMAN

# BECOMING GOD'S WOMAN

Joyce Marie Smith

TYNDALE HOUSE
PUBLISHERS, INC.
WHEATON, ILLINOIS

*To my daughter Lori,
who is in the process
of becoming God's woman*

Bible verses are quoted from *The Living Bible*
© 1971 by Tyndale House Publishers, Inc.,
Wheaton, Illinois

Sixth printing, June 1984

Library of Congress Catalog Card Number 78-57962
ISBN 0-8423-0130-5, paper
Copyright © 1979 by Joyce Marie Smith
All rights reserved
Printed in the United States of America

# CONTENTS

*Preface* 6

### WHO ARE YOU?
1. You Are Special 9
2. Accepting Yourself 13
3. Understanding Yourself 17
4. Your Sexuality 21

### WHO IS GOD?
5. Can You Know God Personally? 27
6. Belonging to God's Family 31
7. The Benefits of Being God's Kid 35
8. How Can You Grow Spiritually? 39

### YOUR RELATIONSHIPS WITH OTHERS
9. How to Make Friends and Be a Friend 45
10. Peer Pressure or Being Cool at School 49
11. How to Be Friends with Your Folks 53
12. Friends with the Opposite Sex 57

*Leader Suggestions and Helps* 61

# PREFACE

The early teen years can be an exciting time of discovery about yourself, other people, your faith, and your world! These years can also be a time of extreme trauma and insecurity.

This study is especially geared to early teen girls (twelve to sixteen) to help make this transition period an adventuresome and happy experience. This study can be used individually or as a group study for home Bible studies, Sunday school classes, youth programs, and D.V.B.S.

# SECTION ONE
# Who Are You?

# LESSON 1

# You Are Special

## Getting Acquainted

1. Draw a picture of who you are, using designs, symbols, and different colors to express your interests (hobbies, sports, activities) and your family. Include your name in your drawing. Share your picture with others and tell them about yourself.

2. Now share one good quality or strength about yourself.

## Why Don't You Feel Special?

*Have someone read the following illustration aloud:*

Betty shuffled slowly down the hall, her eyes downcast and sad. She was lonely and felt rejected by her classmates.

"Nobody likes me," she thought bitterly. "Not only am I fat, but my clothes aren't stylish like everyone else's. And my pimples are so ugly. Who cares that I can make straight A's or play the violin? The guys don't even know I'm alive."

She pulled out a big chocolate bar and munched on it as she brooded over her seemingly hopeless situation.

3. What were Betty's obvious problems? How did her attitudes toward herself affect her behavior? List definite steps Betty could take toward improvement.

_____

_____

_____

Would you like Betty for a friend? How could you help a classmate like Betty? _____

_____

_____

4. What are some other hang-ups teenagers might have in the following categories that would affect their self-image and self-acceptance?

    a. Appearance: _____

    _____

    b. Personality: _____

    _____

    c. Abilities: _____

    _____

    d. Economic background: _____

    _____

    e. Parents and childhood: _____

    _____

## God Made You

5. Read Psalm 139:1-18 aloud, preferably in *The Living Bible*.
   a. What does God know about you? (vv. 1-5) _____

   b. When did God start caring for you? _____

   c. How involved was God in your creation? (vv. 13-16) ___

   d. How does this psalm make you feel? _____

   e. Write out David's prayer in verses 23 and 24. Then pray it aloud. _____

   Yes, God made you. You are special and unique, the only one of a kind. God values you.

## God Loves You

6. Write out John 3:16, using your own name instead of "world" and "anyone" (or "whosoever"). _____

7. Describe God's love as mentioned in these verses:
   a. John 15:9, 13, 14-16 _____
   _____
   b. 1 John 4:9, 10 _____
   c. 1 John 4:16 _____

8. In Jeremiah 31:3 God says, "I have loved you, O my people, with an everlasting love, with lovingkindness I have drawn you to me." How have you experienced God's love?

9. Assignment: Look in the mirror every day this week and say, "God loves me. I love myself."

## Prayer

Thank God that he made you the way you are. Thank him that he loves you and that he has a special plan for you.

# LESSON 2

# Accepting Yourself

## Getting Acquainted

1. Tell about your favorite vacation.
2. Tell something you made or did recently that you are proud of.

## "Not Me, Lord"

*Have two people read the following illustration, one as Moses and one as God:*

"Moses, Moses," God's voice thundered out of the burning bush.

"Who is it?" Moses asked.

"I am the God of your fathers. And I want to send you to set my people free in Egypt. They have been slaves long enough."

"But I can't do that!" Moses exclaimed. "I'm not the person for that job."

"I will be with you, Moses."

"They won't follow me. They won't believe me," Moses cried out.

"I will give you special signs and wonders to show that I have chosen you to lead them."

"But Lord, I'm not a good speaker," Moses stammered.

"Moses, I made your mouth. I will speak through you."

"Lord, please send someone else."

"All right Moses, your brother Aaron will be your spokesman. I will show you what Aaron should tell the people." (See Exodus 3; 4:1, 10-17.)

3. Questions to discuss:
   a. Why was Moses afraid? _____
   b. How did God promise to help him? _____
   _____
   c. Have you ever been afraid of trying something because you felt inferior?
   d. List some things you don't like about yourself.

   _____
   _____
   _____

## Do You Like Yourself?

4. Many teenagers feel inferior. They feel ugly. They feel they are failures.

   Read these Scriptures. How does God view his creation?
   a. Isaiah 45:9 _____

b. Isaiah 64:8 _____

c. Jeremiah 18:1-6 _____

_____

Should you reject what God has made? What are you telling God if you are unhappy with yourself?

5. Our self-image is a result of how we accept our looks, abilities, personality, and home life, how we think others look at us, and how others have treated us in the past. Learn to accept the things you can't change about yourself.

## The Big Put-down

Do you know someone who is always complaining or talks negatively? Do you like to be around him or her? If you have developed a habit of thinking negatively about yourself, ask God to help change your thoughts. Don't put yourself down!

## God's Values

6. In our culture, physical beauty, intelligence, and money are top priorities. But God has a set of values different from that of the world. List God's values in these verses.

   a. Psalm 1:6 _____
   b. Proverbs 31:30 _____
   c. Hebrews 11:6 _____
   d. 1 Peter 3:3, 4 _____

7. List specific ways these qualities of inner beauty and spiritual depth can be developed in your life. _____

_____

_____

## Develop Yourself!

8. In what areas (such as music, sports, leadership, hobbies and crafts, clubs, youth program at church, etc.) are you developing your abilities and skills? By developing your strengths, you compensate for your weaknesses. This helps build a good self-image. You'll like yourself better as you begin to excel in something.

9. Philippians 1:6 says God is at work in our lives. Don't get discouraged over mistakes and failures. God is helping you develop and grow through these experiences. Share about an area of your life in which you feel God is working right now.

## Prayer

Father, there are some things I really don't like about myself. But there are some things that I do like. Help me to work on those areas in which I feel inferior and to appreciate my strengths.

And Father, thank you for loving me and making me special.

# LESSON 3

# Understanding Yourself

## Getting Acquainted

1. Name one person who has had an influence on you besides your parents.

2. Describe who and what you are today.

## Who Am I?

3. When we are born we come into the world with inherited looks (color of eyes, hair, bone structure, height, etc.) and a basic temperament. Each person develops his own personality. How would you define personality? _____
_____

17

4. Here are four different types of people:
    a. Susie is a popular girl and loves to be with people. She is an extrovert. She is happy and cheerful. She is loving. She is usually disorganized, however, and has many unfinished projects in her room. She is emotional and cries easily. She may get angry but forgives and forgets.
    b. Melanie is a faithful and loyal friend. She tends to be shy. She is a hard worker and is very dependable and responsible. She is a talented artist and musician. She usually enjoys reading and quiet activities. Melanie is self-centered, though, and is easily hurt. She can be gloomy, negative, and moody.
    c. Cathy is a born leader. She is self-confident and likes to be involved in many activities. She is very organized and easily makes decisions. She is optimistic and adventuresome. Cathy has a temper, though. She tends to be bossy and is insensitive to others. She likes to dominate.
    d. Paula is calm, easygoing, dependable, and stable. She tends to be quiet. Paula has a dry sense of humor and enjoys poking fun at people. She is a peacemaker and a good listener. Paula tends to be lazy, though, and lets others do the work. She can be selfish and stubborn.

Do you see yourself pictured by one of these types of temperaments? Maybe you are a mixture of several of these types.

5. List some of your strengths and weaknesses.

| *Strengths* | *Weaknesses* |
|---|---|
| | |
| | |
| | |

Thank God for your strengths.
Circle two weaknesses you will work on this week.

## Emotions

6. Besides your own personality characteristics, there are other factors that influence your reactions. Circumstances (such as failing a test), people around you (such as a teacher or parent who yells at you), the weather (a depressing fog or a violent storm), and your physical condition (a bad cold or poor health), all influence and affect your emotions. Can you add any others? _____

_____

As girls enter adolescence and develop physically, hormonal changes also influence their emotions. During adolescence your feelings are more intense and deep—you may be explosive and sensitive. You may cry easily. You may be up today and down tomorrow. Your emotions fluctuate frequently.

7. Circle the emotions you have the most problems with:

| anger | hate | bitterness | impatience |
| fear | worry | guilt | depression |
| jealousy | self-pity | | |

Ask God to help you overcome these problems.

8. Read 1 Corinthians 13:4-7. What are the characteristics of love? _____

What two or three characteristics would you like to have? What are some other positive emotions you would like to develop? _____

_____

_____

## Dreams, Aspirations, and Purpose

9. List several plans and dreams you have for the future.

_____
_____
_____
_____

Do you have any idea what type of job or profession you would like to prepare for?

10. Pick two of the following people and tell how they used their lives for the Lord.
   a. Esther (Esther 4:14; 7:3, 4)
   b. Joseph (Genesis 45:4-8)
   c. Moses (Exodus 3:6-10)
   d. Deborah (Judges 4:4-8)
   e. Mary (Matthew 1:18-24)
   f. Paul (Acts 9:15)

_____
_____
_____
_____
_____

Name one adult you know today that you admire and would like to imitate or use as a model for your life. _____
_____

## Prayer

Pray a sentence prayer, asking God to help you in one area of your life.

## LESSON 4

# Your Sexuality

## Getting Acquainted

1. Are there any times you wished you were the opposite sex? When? Why?

2. What is the importance of accepting your sex?

## God's Plan

During these days of emphasis on unisex it is important to understand why God created two sexes. God did have a beautiful plan and purpose in mind!

3. In Genesis 1:26, 27, how were man and woman created equal? _____

4. In Genesis 2:18, 20, what reason is given for woman's creation? _____
(Compare with 1 Corinthians 11:9.)

5. From Genesis 3:16, who was to be the head of the home?
_____
(Compare with Ephesians 5:22, 23.)

The husband has been likened to the president of a corporation and the wife to the vice-president. They are equal in importance and status, but different in position and responsibilities.

6. First Corinthians 11:11 says, "But remember that in God's plan, men and women need each other." Man and woman are to be dependent upon each other and mutually submissive (Ephesians 5:21).

How do you think your parents (or another couple you know) *complement* each other? _____
_____

## Developing Your Sexuality

Rather than get hung up on rights and roles and rebelling, begin to realize the importance of developing your *character* as an importart part of your sexuality.

7. How would you define femininity? (Think of a woman you really admire.) _____
_____

8. Describe these six women mentioned in Proverbs:
   a. Wise (Proverbs 14:1; 31:26, 30, 31) _____
   _____

b. Foolish (14:1; 20:3) _____
   c. Gracious (11:16; 31:26) _____
   d. Contentious (19:13; 21:9, 19; 27:15, 16) _____
   
   _____
   
   e. Virtuous (12:4; 31:10) _____
   f. Sensuous (2:16-19; 5:3-6; 6:23-26; 7:6-12) _____
   
   _____

Which women do you most desire to be like and why? Which type would you like to have for a friend? List several specific things you plan to do to become more like them. _____

_____

_____


## Developing Physically

9. *Your body.* What exercise does your body get? Describe ways you take care of your body. _____

_____

10. *Food.* What wholesome foods do you regularly eat for a healthy body? What foods should you stay away from? _____

_____

11. *Clothes.* Your appearance tells a lot about you. How do you feel about your appearance? Where do you need to improve? _____

_____

In Lesson 12 we will discuss further the moral problems regarding your sexuality.

## Application

1. The total acceptance of the sex that God gave you is extremely important for your happiness and fulfillment as a person.

2. Don't try to compete with the opposite sex to prove you are as good or better—just concentrate on developing yourself.

# SECTION TWO
# Who Is God?

# LESSON 5

# Can You Know God Personally?

## Getting Acquainted

Can you imagine the thrill of being ushered into the presence of the President of the United States? And of having him address you by name, talk with you, express his love and concern for you, and get to know you personally?

Now, can you imagine the possibility of knowing God, the Creator of the world, in a personal way? Is it possible?

1. Describe your idea of God. How do you picture him?

## Is God for Real?

2. There are several ways we can know God is for real.

   a. First, *creation* itself is a proof of God's existence. Read Psalm 19:1-6. Do you believe there is a Creator? _____ (Compare Genesis 1 with Romans 1:19, 20.)

   Describe a time when you could see God's handiwork around you. Did it make you feel close to God? How?

   _____

   _____

   b. Second, *God's Word* reveals God to us. Read Psalm 19:7-11. How does the Bible reveal God to us? _____

   _____

   How does God's Word speak to you? _____

   _____

   c. Third, *God personally speaks* to us and reveals himself. Can you think of any Bible examples of God speaking to men personally? _____

   _____

   How has God spoken directly to you? _____

   _____

   Romans 2:15 says each man has a conscience. How does God speak through our consciences? _____

   _____

   d. Fourth, God's Son, *Jesus Christ,* reveals God to us. Read John 1:1, 2, 14. Who does it say Jesus is? _____ John 12:45 says, "For when you see me, you are seeing the one who sent me."

## One Way

3. In John 14:6 Jesus says that the only way we can come to God is through Jesus Christ. Jesus said he was the _____, the _____, and the _____. Read verses 6-10 and explain them in your own words.

4. Who do these people say Jesus is?

   |  | Person | Statement |
   |---|---|---|
   | a. Matthew 16:15, 16 | | |
   | b. Mark 1:10, 11 | | |
   | c. John 1:32-34 | | |
   | d. John 1:47-49 | | |
   | e. John 11:25-27 | | |

   Who do you say Jesus is? _____

## God in Person

Colossians 2:9 says, "For in Christ there is all of God in a human body." Hebrews 1:3a says, "God's Son shines out with God's glory, and all that God's Son is and does marks him as God."

In John 10:30 Jesus claims to be equal to God.

5. What are some characteristics of God that Jesus showed us when he walked on planet Earth? _____

6. Let's try some charades. Divide into two or three groups. Each group take one of the following Scriptures: John 2:1-11;

John 6:1-14; John 6:16-21; and John 5:1-9. *Have each group take turns acting out their story of Jesus while the others try to guess what it is.*

What does this story tell us about Jesus? _____

_____

How does it affect you? _____

_____

7. Optional: Draw a poster expressing who God is to you, using symbols and words (such as the cross, fish, dove, rainbow, and words such as peace, love, joy, etc.).

## Prayer

Close this time with sentence prayers, thanking God for the way he reveals himself to us.

## LESSON 6

# Belonging to God's Family

### Getting Acquainted

Share something special about belonging to your family.

### People Who Met Jesus

*Divide the class into three or four small groups. Have each group read the Scripture and answer the questions. Each small group should summarize their findings for the class.*

1. The Woman of Samaria (John 4:7-39)
   a. Why did the woman of Samaria need Christ? (vv. 13-18)

   _____

   _____

   b. How did she react to Christ? (vv. 19, 29) _____

_____

   c. What was the result of her testimony? (vv. 28-30, 39)

_____

2. Paul (Saul) (Acts 9:1-22)
   a. Who spoke to Paul on the road to Damascus? (vv. 4, 5)

_____

   b. What did Paul say of Christ? (vv. 20, 22) _____

_____

   c. What became Paul's mission in life? (vv. 15, 16) \_\_\_\_\_

_____

3. Peter (Luke 5:1-11)
   a. When Jesus began catching so many fish, what was Peter's reaction? (vv. 8, 9) _____
     Why? _____
   b. How did Peter respond to Jesus' call? (vv. 10, 11)

_____

   c. What resulted from Peter's first sermon? See Acts 2:38-41. _____

_____

_____

(Other Scriptures you could use: Thomas—John 20:24-29; Martha—John 11:1-4, 17-27.)

Conclusion: These people all experienced changes when they met Jesus as their Savior. Others could see the difference in their lives.

4. Would you like to share your experience of accepting Christ as your Savior? What difference has Christ made in your life?

## God's Family

God wants to adopt each one of us into his family. As his children we are eligible for a spiritual inheritance. He has a storehouse of gifts, abilities, and talents for us. He has a beautiful plan for each one of our lives, and he wants to give us fulfillment and purpose here on earth. After life on earth he promises us a home in heaven with him.

## Would You Like to Belong to the Family of God?

5. First, you must realize your need for God.
    Read Romans 3:23. Who has sinned? _____
That includes you!

When we study the characteristics of God we see that he is good, righteous, just, and holy. Our sin keeps us from his presence and from fellowshiping with him.

Romans 6:23 tells us the result of our sin: _____

List some of your sins. _____

_____

6. Because of God's love he provided a way for us to be forgiven and have fellowship with him. John 3:16 says God gave so we would have _____

_____.

Romans 5:8 says Christ _____ _____ _____.

1 John 4:9, 10 says God sent _____

_____.

Christ not only died for us but rose from the grave (1 Corinthians 15:3, 4). He is alive today!

7. By accepting Christ as your own Savior you can become God's child and receive forgiveness.

John 1:12 says I must _____ him and _____ on his name.

Ephesians 2:8, 9 says we are saved by _____, not works.

Revelation 3:20 says I must _____.

8. Are you sorry for your sins? Are you ready to ask Christ to forgive you and cleanse you?

## Prayer

Lord, I admit my need for you. I confess that I have sinned. Thank you that you died for me and have forgiven me. I want you to come into my life as my Savior and Lord. In Jesus' name, Amen.

LESSON 7

# The Benefits of Being God's Kid

## Getting Acquainted

1. Share some benefits of being a member of your family. There are some exciting benefits of belonging to God's family, too.

## Assurance

2. Last week you may have become a Christian by confessing your sin and asking Christ to come into your life. How do you know for sure you are a believer?

   a. 1 John 5:11-13 says you have _____
   _____

   b. Philippians 1:6 says God is continuing his _____ in you.

c. From Revelation 3:20, where is Christ now? _____

Our faith is based on the *fact* of God's Word, not on how we *feel*.

## A New Friend

3. Jesus says he is now your friend (John 15:15). What are some advantages of having Jesus for your friend? _____

_____

What one condition is given in our friendship with Jesus (John 15:14)? _____

## Guilt

4. Guilt over past sins and mistakes can make you feel ashamed and can affect your self-image. As God's child, when you sin you are _____ and _____ (1 John 1:9). Once you have confessed your sin, you are totally forgiven.

5. Look at these promises:
   a. Isaiah 44:22 says God blots out our sins like a thick cloud.
   b. Psalm 103:12 says he removes them from us as far as the east is from the west.
   c. Micah 7:19 says he casts them into the depths of the deepest sea. (Corrie ten Boom reminds us that God puts a "No Fishing Allowed" over the spot—he doesn't want us to drag them back up.)
   d. Jeremiah 31:34 promises us that he remembers our sins no more.

6. To continue to feel guilty over a sin God has already forgiven is to call him a liar. Pause for a moment of silent prayer,

confessing your sins to God. Thank him for forgiving you. If you continue to feel guilty after confessing your sin, realize this is not God condemning you (Romans 8:1), but Satan, who accuses us (Revelation 12:10). Reject those thoughts from our enemy Satan.

7. Share an example of when you have sinned against someone else and have needed to ask that person to forgive you. Read Mark 11:25, 26. Do you need to ask anyone to forgive you? Write their name here.

---

## God's Promises—Part of Your Inheritance

*Suggestion: Divide the class into several small groups. Have them look up the Scriptures and match up the answers. Discuss the answers with personal illustrations if possible.*

8. Directions: Draw a line connecting the Scripture reference with the proper answer.

| | | |
|---|---|---|
| a. | Psalm 32:8 | abundant life |
| b. | Isaiah 41:10 | guidance |
| c. | Psalm 50:15 | strength |
| d. | John 10:10 | love, other character qualities |
| e. | John 14:27 | his presence; no fear |
| f. | Philippians 4:13 | peace |
| g. | Matthew 11:28, 29 | deliverance |
| h. | Galatians 5:22, 23 | rest |
| i. | Acts 1:8 | protection |
| j. | Hebrews 13:5 | victory |
| k. | Psalm 34:7 | power to witness |
| l. | 1 Corinthians 15:57 | never fails or leaves us |
| m. | John 16:24 | help in temptations |

(cont.)

n. 1 Corinthians 10:13   wisdom
o. Philippians 4:19      answered prayer
p. James 1:5             provides your needs

## Prayer

Stop right now and pray sentence prayers, thanking God for one particular promise (or asking God to provide for one of your needs).

LESSON 8

# How Can You Grow Spiritually?

## Getting Acquainted

Have you ever seen a mentally retarded person in an adult body, with the mind and IQ of a baby or small child? It's a sad sight, isn't it? It's just as sad to see a Christian who does not grow and mature, but is weak and helpless and dependent.

## How Can You Grow?

1. Study your Bible!
   "Be a good workman, one who does not need to be ashamed when God examines your work. Know what his Word says and means" (2 Timothy 2:15).

God has given us a road map for our journey through life—the Bible. It shows us how to live and make decisions, what God's standards are for us, and what God himself is like. It shows us examples of how to live by looking at other people's mistakes and victories. It helps us believe in Jesus.

a. In a few words, write out each of these promises connected with reading God's Word.

Psalm 119:9, 11 _____

Joshua 1:8 _____

1 Peter 2:2, 3 _____

God wants us to read the Bible, study, memorize, and meditate upon it. He also wants us to *obey* his Word.

b. Share what you are doing for devotions or Bible study.
c. Try to read some Scripture each day. See how long it takes to read the book of John; then try the whole New Testament.
d. Some time this week do a simple Bible study by using Psalm 1 and listing: Commands to Obey; Promises to Claim; Sins to Forsake; and Examples to Follow.

2. Talk to God.

"Don't worry about anything; instead, pray about everything; tell God your needs and don't forget to thank him for his answers" (Philippians 4:6).

*Kinds of Prayer:*

a. Worship and praise.
   Worship expresses our love to God. List some things you are thankful for about God and what he has done for you. (Read Psalm 100 if you have time.) _____

_____

_____

Using sentence prayers, take some time to thank God right now for some things you are thankful for.

b. Confession of sins.

Even the smallest sin can stand between us and God and keep our prayers from being answered. (Read Psalm 51 if you have time.) Confess your sins in short sentence prayers.

c. Petitions for your own needs.

Nothing is too big or too small to bring to God! List some of your needs, then bring them to God. _____

_____

Begin a prayer notebook with these headings:

*Date*     *Request*     *Date Answered*

d. Intercession for others.

As you pray for others you release God's power and blessing. List requests and then pray for friends, family, church, and our country.

3. Fellowship with other Christians.

"Let us not neglect our church meetings as some people do, but encourage and warn each other" (Hebrews 10:25).

Discuss the reasons for going to church; for fellowshiping with other believers; for being involved in a Christian organization such as Teen Dimension, Campus Life, or Young Life.

Are you regularly going to church? _____
If not, why not? _____

4. Witness for Christ by your life and words.
   a. Why? (Romans 10:9, 10) _____
   _____

   b. How? (1 Peter 3:15) _____
   _____

List two people you want to share Christ with. Begin praying for them.

_____
_____

## Prayer

Ask God to help you discipline yourself to spend time every day reading his instructions for your life.

SECTION THREE
# Your Relationship with Others

**LESSON 9**

# How to Make Friends and Be a Friend

## Getting Acquainted

1. Write down the names of your three closest friends.

___

Think of several others you also like to be with.

2. List what you especially like about these friends.

___

Share the characteristics that are most important to you in your friendships.

## Being a Friend

3. Do you know the best way to make a friend? *Be a friend!*
   Discuss these suggestions for being a good friend. Add a few of your own.
   
   a. Never make fun of your friend or put him or her down. (Don't be cutting or mean; don't ridicule.)
   b. Don't gossip about your friend to others. Keep confidences.
   c. Accept your friend as he or she is—don't try to change him or her.
   d. Don't become possessive of your friend or jealous of his or her friendship with others.
   e. Be sensitive to your friend's needs.
   f. Be interested in your friend—his or her home life, activities, etc.
   g. _____
   h. _____
   i. _____

4. How does the Golden Rule ("Do unto others as you would have them do unto you") apply in friendships?

5. Read 1 Corinthians 13:4-7 (in *The Living Bible*) and list the qualities of a loving friend. _____
   _____
   _____

6. How does the Bible describe a good friend?
   a. Proverbs 17:17 _____
   b. Proverbs 18:24 _____
   c. Proverbs 17:9 _____

## Influences—for Good or Evil

7. Who are we told *not* to have as our friends?
   a. Proverbs 22:5 _____
   b. Proverbs 22:24, 25 _____
   c. Proverbs 23:19, 20 _____
   d. Proverbs 23:26, 27 _____
   e. James 4:4 _____

8. One of the most important decisions you make as a teenager is whom you choose for your friends. They influence your behavior (actions, language, activities), standards (dress, morality), and basic philosophy (godly or ungodly). You become like your friends.

   Name two ways you have been influenced by your group of friends. _____
   _____
   _____

9. What kind of an influence do you have on your friends?
   a. Do you witness to your friends about what God means to you?
   b. Do you invite your friends to church or Christian organizations?
   c. Do you stand up for what you believe—your values and standards and beliefs?

## Application

1. If you feel you need a close friend, begin praying for one. Ask God to help you be a friend to someone.

2. Are you trying to become a better friend to others as suggested in question 3?

3. Is there someone with whom you should discontinue your friendship because of his or her bad influence (as discussed in questions 7 and 8)?

4. Try to do something (as suggested in question 9) to have a good influence on your friends.

## Prayer

Pray, asking God to help you be a good friend and to stay away from relationships that are not good for you.

# LESSON 10

# Peer Pressure or Being Cool at School

## Getting Acquainted

Illustration: Barbara is riding around town with some friends. Claudia pulls out a joint (or it could be alcohol, LSD, or other drugs) and offers one to Barbara. Barbara doesn't want to take one but is on the spot.

How do you think Barbara feels? Why?
How could she turn down the offer?

## Conformed or Transformed

1. How do teenagers conform? Discuss ways you conform
   a. physically: _____
   _____

b. socially: _____

   c. morally: _____

   d. spiritually: _____

2. Why do teenagers conform to peer pressure?
   a. Fear of being ridiculed or laughed at
   b. Desire to be like everyone else; fear of being different
   c. Desire to grow up and be away from parents
   d. Lack of self-confidence; or low self-image

3. Results of conforming to peer pressure:
   a. Developing a habit you will regret later
   b. Making a harmful decision
   c. Compromising your standards

   Remember, your group will actually respect someone who takes a stand for what she believes—it shows she has guts.

4. What does Romans 12:1, 2 tell us about conforming to the world? _____

5. Last time we discussed friendships. How are your friends influencing you right now? _____

   Did you make any changes in your friendships after last time?

6. The Bible teaches that we are to be *in* the world but not *of* the world (John 17:14).

a. 1 Corinthians 5:9-11 says we are not to keep company with _____.
b. 2 Corinthians 6:14-18 says we are to be _____ from unrighteous people.
c. Ephesians 5:11 says not to fellowship with _____
_____.
d. 2 Timothy 2:22 says to flee from _____
_____.

## Decisions, Decisions

Sometimes at school or with friends you are faced with a decision regarding your behavior, activities, or standards. You need to know ahead of time what God's principles are for making decisions.

7. Draw lines matching the phrase with the correct Scripture.
   a. 1 Corinthians 6:19    Don't cause someone to stumble.
   b. Romans 14:13          Your body belongs to Christ.
   c. 1 Corinthians 10:31   You are to obey your parents.
   d. Colossians 3:20       You are to glorify Christ.

8. One helpful technique in making a decision is to list advantages (reasons for) and disadvantages (reasons against) in two columns and compare them.

9. There are hundreds of commands in the Bible that also tell us how to live. If you want to know God's will in a specific area:
   a. Look for some Scripture—a command or promise
   b. Pray about it—ask God's wisdom and direction
   c. Ask for the inner peace of the Holy Spirit

d. Ask God to work through circumstances (an open or shut door)
   e. Seek counsel from Christian friends and leaders

10. If your friends are trying to influence you to do something, ask yourself:
    a. Is it healthy and good for my body?
    b. Does it help me be a better witness?
    c. What does the Bible say about it?
    d. Can I say, "Thank you Lord for _____"?

## Prayer

Have a time of sentence prayers for each other. Ask the Lord to help each of you to be strong in temptation and to make the right decisions. Pray that you will have the right friends. Ask the Lord to help you take a stand for what you believe.

# LESSON 11

# How to Be Friends with Your Folks

### Getting Acquainted

1. Share one thing you appreciate most about your parents.

2. Share two rules in your home—one rule you agree with and one rule you think is unfair.

### Game Rules

Every home needs *game rules*—standards for behavior. Can you imagine watching a football game in which there were no rules?

As a teenager develops her independence, she still needs

rules and guidelines regarding her responsibilities at home, relationships with others, activities, friends, and later in driving and dating. Boundaries and disciplines give a sense of security and love. One teenager complained, "Yeah, my folks really loved me a lot! I sure got a lot of spankings as a kid!"

It helps to sit down and discuss the rules with your parents. It might even be good to write down the standards your family decides upon so everyone knows exactly what is expected and why.

3. What command is given to children?
   a. Exodus 20:12 _____
   b. Ephesians 6:1-3 _____
   c. Colossians 3:20 _____

4. Does it say there are any exceptions to this rule? _____
   What do you think "honor your parents" means?

## Communication: Listening and Talking

5. Are you and your parents able to discuss differences together? Circle Y (yes) or N (no) for the following questions:

Y  N  Do you feel your parents usually understand you?
Y  N  Are you able to tell your parents how you feel?
Y  N  Do your parents put you down or belittle you?
Y  N  Quarreling and arguing can be helpful. Do you agree?
Y  N  If you don't get your way do you have a temper tantrum?
Y  N  Can nagging and faultfinding help you have good behavior?

6. List two subjects you would like to discuss with your parents. _____

_____

What is preventing this discussion? _____

7. What are some good guidelines in communication? Draw a line from the Scripture to the appropriate phrase.

   a. James 1:19         Don't decide before knowing facts.
   b. Ephesians 4:31, 32  Listen much, speak little.
   c. Proverbs 18:13     Don't quarrel but be forgiving.
   d. Proverbs 17:9      Fools argue and become angry.
   e. Mark 11:25         Don't nag.
   f. Proverbs 29:8, 11   Truth is best.
   g. Proverbs 12:14, 19  Forgive each other.

Circle the Scriptures you especially need in *your* life.

8. Name two main things you and your parents argue and disagree over. _____

_____

What can you do to resolve these conflicts? _____

## The Hardest Words to Say

Six of the hardest words to say are "I'm sorry. Will you forgive me?" An important part of any healthy relationship is learning to forgive each other and not allowing hostility and bitterness to develop.

9. What commands are given regarding forgiveness?
    a. Matthew 5:23, 24 _____
    b. Ephesians 4:31, 32 _____

Mark 11:26 reminds us of the importance of forgiving, "But if you do not forgive, neither will your Father in heaven forgive your failings and shortcomings."

When you refuse to forgive someone else you make it impossible for God to forgive you, because you cannot receive that forgiveness.

Can you think of any examples in the Bible of forgiveness? Do you need to ask anyone for forgiveness?


## Application

1. How do you show love for your parents?

2. Name one way you are going to change in your relationship with your parents.

3. Are you trying to discuss things with them more?


## Prayer

Praise God for what he has done for you; ask forgiveness for any sin in your life (especially toward parents); ask for the Lord's help in being a better daughter; pray for your friends.

## LESSON 12

# Friends with the Opposite Sex

### Getting Acquainted

You are discovering the wonderful world of the opposite sex. Suddenly you find yourself intrigued and fascinated with this new discovery. It is healthy to make friends with guys. But you may have some questions in this area or be unsure of what kind of relationship to have.

### Friends

1. How can you feel at ease with the opposite sex?
   a. What are some topics you could discuss? _____
   _____
   _____
   _____

b. How can you show your interest in the other person?

_____
_____
_____

c. What is the difference between friendliness and flirting?

_____
_____
_____

## Dating and Standards

2. List several rules and standards your parents have for dating. _____
_____
_____

The best way to start dating is with a group. Why? List several activities (places to go, things to do) that would be good ideas for dates. _____
_____

List possible places or amusements to avoid. _____
_____

How can the way a girl dresses help or hinder a guy? _____
_____

## Sex Drive

The sex drive affects boys so that they are very interested in the *bodies* of girls, whereas girls are more interested in boys' *personalities* and mannerisms. Suddenly a whole new world of emotions and desires can erupt in close physical contact.

Perhaps you are asked or encouraged to do something physically together. How do you know what is right?

3. What reason is given in 1 Corinthians 6:15-20 for keeping your body pure? _____

4. In 1 Thessalonians 4:3-5, what is God's will for you?

_____

5. In Galatians 5:19-21, what sexual sins are listed?

_____

6. When does Hebrews 13:4 say the sex act is OK?

_____

If God created this drive, how can it be sin? Within the protection, security, and love of a permanent marriage relationship, the sexual act is a beautiful and unifying experience. Outside of marriage it is destructive, and leads to the following problems:

*Physically:* venereal disease, pregnancy

*Emotionally and mentally:* guilt, insecurity, mistrust, a low self-image and loss of self-respect, a feeling of being used.

*Spiritually:* as sin it breaks fellowship with God and hardens the heart.

God loves you and wants to protect you. That is why he doesn't want you to have sex before marriage. It is important that you develop strong convictions and moral standards *before* you actually are faced with the temptation. Don't be caught off guard.

## Facing Temptation

One of Satan's main means of tempting teenagers to sin is in the area of sex and immorality. He tempts you to sin through your thoughts, desires, and finally your actions.

7. Can you think of any Bible characters who faced sexual temptations? How did they handle them? What were the results?

_____

_____

8. What does God promise to us as we face temptations?
   a. 1 Corinthians 10:13 _____
   b. James 4:7 _____
   c. 2 Peter 2:9 _____

9. How are we to react to temptations?
   a. Matthew 26:41 _____
   b. Ephesians 6:16 _____
   c. 1 Peter 5:8, 9 _____

10. What do these Scriptures say about forgiveness when you do sin or fail?
   a. Psalm 51 _____
   b. 1 John 1:7-9 _____
   (Also, review lesson 7.)

## Prayer

Close with sentence prayers, asking God to help you maintain physical purity, and to develop the right friends and standards.

# LEADER SUGGESTIONS AND HELPS

## General

1. Serve refreshments as you begin each week to encourage a relaxed, informal atmosphere.

2. If the girls are at different stages of spiritual growth, it might be better to do the lesson together. If they are all fairly mature spiritually, they could prepare ahead. However, it seems best to have either one plan or the other.

3. Encourage them to use their Bible's table of contents if they have trouble finding a passage. It helps if everyone has the same translation (preferably *The Living Bible,* or another modern translation). Be ready to call out page numbers if needed.

4. When there is a group of Scriptures in the lesson, have volunteers read them rather than having everyone look up each verse.

5. The "Getting Acquainted" sections are just that—to encourage participation on a nonthreatening basis. Encourage everyone to share a thought or comment.

6. Encourage a prayer time at the end of each lesson, especially from lesson 6 on. Use short, specific, honest sentence prayers. Use a prayer list to keep track of answered prayers.

7. These lessons are planned for approximately a forty-five-minute study but can be adapted for a longer or shorter session. To shorten, cut out some of the discussion questions, have a very short prayer time, and no refreshments.

8. Older teen girls might find the Bible study *Fulfillment* more pertinent.

## Specific

Lesson 1
You will need white art (construction) paper, crayons or colored pencils. For background material on lessons 1 and 2, use the tapes *Preparing for Adolescence* by Dr. James Dobson, One Way Library, 1507 E. McFadden, Santa Ana, CA 92705. Other good reference material would include *Hide or Seek* by James Dobson, (Old Tappan, NJ: Revell, 1974); and *Do I Have to Be Me?* by Lloyd Ahlem (Glendale, CA: Regal, 1981).

Lesson 2
Reference book: *Thank God I'm a Teenager* by Charles Mueller and Donald Bardill (Minncapolis, MN: Augsburg Publishing House, 1976).

Lesson 3
You could ask four different people to read the four personality types. Reference book: *Spirit-Controlled Temperament* by Tim LaHaye (Wheaton, IL: Tyndale, 1966).

Lesson 4
Reference book: *Fulfilled Marriage* by Norman Wright (Irvine, CA: Harvest House, 1976).

Lesson 5
For the poster (if you have time) you will need construction paper, crayons, etc.

Lesson 6
You could use the Four Spiritual Laws booklet by Campus Crusade instead of questions 5-7.

Lesson 7
Reference book: *The Guilt Trip* by Hal Lindsey (Grand Rapids, MI: Zondervan, 1973).

Lesson 8
The *Youth Bible Study Notebook* by John Souter (Wheaton, IL: Tyndale, 1977) would be a good book to encourage them to use on their own.

Lesson 9
Reference book: *So You're a Teenage Girl* by Jill Renich (Grand Rapids, MI: Zondervan, 1966).

Lesson 10
Refer to Dobson tapes: also *Dare to Discipline* by James Dobson (Wheaton, IL: Tyndale, 1970).

Lesson 12
Use the Dobson tapes.